Poetic Justice, Speak!

Can They Hear Us?

Carol Hurst

REJOICE
Essential Publishing

Carol Hurst/Rejoice Essential Publishing

PO BOX 512

Effingham, SC 29541

www.republishing.org

Unless otherwise indicated, scripture is taken from the King James Version.

Scripture quotations marked (NIV) are taken from the Holy Bible, New International Version®, NIV®. Copyright © 1973, 1978, 1984, 2011 by Biblica, Inc.™ Used by permission of Zondervan. All rights reserved worldwide. www.zondervan.comThe "NIV" and "New International Version" are trademarks registered in the United States Patent and Trademark Office by Biblica, Inc.™

Poetic Justice, Speak!/Carol Hurst

ISBN-13: 978-1-956775-57-0

The book is dedicated to the ones that are in physical or mental captivity all over the world. Are we paying attention?

Out in the open, wisdom calls aloud. She raises her voice in the public square; on top of the wall, she cries out; at the city gate, she makes her speech.—Proverbs 1:20-21(NIV)

Selah

Preface

As you read these poems, my friend, I hope you become more aware of your surroundings and not become judgmental when you think someone is acting out of the norm. We often miss vital evidence of the captured, suicidal, and unloved. Why? Because we are not focused on anyone but ourselves. Have you ever been in a situation where if you had said or done something, it would have turned out another way? Did you miss the chance out of fear or avoid getting involved? Well, I have composed some insightful poetry for us to take a closer look the next time we see signs and think twice before looking away.

Content

1

I Know You're Out There.

Do you hear the screams?
The one that has a dream.
Just like me, who long to be free.
Confused about what is happening.
I scream, "Can you hear me?"
I will call until you come.
It doesn't matter where you are from.
I will wait forcefully in my fear,
Until someone comes and the road is clear.
If I die before I wake
Please come save me, before it's too late.
I am depending on you,
Do not ignore me too.

I am waiting.

2

Absolutely Ignored

My friends tried to warn me,
How you fought for your life, helplessly.
Give me a minute or maybe an hour.
I just got off work and taking a shower.
The baby is crying, and she wants to play.
If I tell her no, there is hell to pay.
I heard screams and saw them on the news.
I couldn't believe my eyes and said, "How rude."
Hold on for a minute; the phone is ringing.
It's my mom. She is so clingy.
She kept talking and I tried to hang up.
I must have dozed off,
By then, it was time to get up.
I heard your screams, but not the sound.
You lived in the basement underground.

My schedule was so busy.
I am vomiting guilt and a tortured conscience.

3

In the Dumpster

The dumpster is full of things.
I even smell the hint of wings.
The sauce slowly dripped down my face.
At the same time, they're trying to close my case.
Helpless, I lie under a bag of glass,
moving from place to place.
My eyes have no vision because my predator cut my face.
If you walk over near the grocery store,
 you'll see my pink lace.
Hurry, please help me before they close this case.
I'm losing my conscience and my thoughts more day by day.
One thing that I know, God is here with me
 and now it's time to pray.
Someone is coming; let them know I am in here.

4

Homeless Man Happened

My life is good; I don't see any danger or change in sight.

I park my car in the driveway in the middle of the night.

I walked into the house, happy as I could be,

My wife stared in horror,

They just revoked the lease.

As she screamed and called out my name at that point, I began to cry.

When I looked up to tell her, "I love her,"

she walked away and said good-bye.

I dropped my head and stomped my feet; I didn't know what to do.

She grabbed her keys, then the baby, and said, "I'm taking the money too."

I grabbed my phone, checked the accounts

that set us up for life.

I stood there broken when all at once,

I have no money in sight.

At that point, my home became the street.

Please help me. I am on my way to the bridge to jump.

 Please save me when you see me walking.

5

Shine The Light Over Here. Hurry!

I hear the cars passing behind the shack in the field.
It's only 20 feet away, on the side of the hill.
Where is everyone going? The cars are moving so fast.
Can someone stop to take a leap and maybe run out of gas?
By surprise, someone stopped; I heard singing and laugher.
But no one bothered to look in the shack to see how badly
he stabbed her.
Please help us; we are innocent, just like you.
We were happy the way we were, young and going to school.
This is mentally draining.
I am losing myself, and my sense of reality is gone.
Please hear our cry; we just want to go home!

5 SHINE THE LIGHT OVER HERE. HURRY!

SHHHH! Here they come; please help my unconscious friend and I!

6

Warning! Mentally Disturbed

I look customary to you and everyone else,
That does not know this house is a living hell.
I must look the part as I go out the door,
Cause if I don't, my head will hit the floor.
Help me; look deep into my eyes, and you will see the truth,
Then take a glimpse of my neck and back; you will see the bruise.
Can someone hear the thunder as the night began to roar?
The screams of brutality and swinging fists, being called a whore.
 I hear music and laughter; everyone is having a good time.

Only two steps away, I duck every second from objects thrown like a wind chime.   I can't take this anymore; the beatings are hard to bear.

It feels like an innocent dream, that turned into a nightmare. I'm going nowhere.

When the abuse is over in the morning, please hear my cry.
I will drive myself to an end; stop me; I don't want to die.
The seabed is waiting for me! Hurry!!

7

In The Trunk!

I did not want to take this ride; I was snatched on this summer's day.

I only think about holding my dolls and going out to play.

My life has taken a different turn, and things I can't comprehend,

I know that I love my parents, brothers, and friends.

I know they wonder what happened and why I'm not at the dinner table.

Do they know I'm down the street, tied with tape and cables?

Do not overlook me; here I am, trying to scream and fight.

The more I move and kick the rope, they get tighter and tighter.

I hear the sirens coming toward me and hear my dad too.

The sound seemed to fade away as he drove closer to the loop.

7 IN THE TRUNK!

Hurry, someone catches me before I get away.
If you don't, I'll be a memory soon fading away.
Do it now. I am not just a case number. Move quickly.

8

Show Real Love Next Time

I love you is a cliché; it's something you must do.

 I knew it was not natural from the time I laid eyes on you.

Back and forth, forth and back, was a theme for you each day.

Ignoring my genuine love is a price you will have to pay.

Someone comes and helps me; I'm in desperate need of attention.

Before I do something stupid, and things I don't want to mention.

I crave your attention wanting your touch more and more.

You treat me like a stranger, then call me a whore.

You held the key to my heart that no one else could take.

I gave three more men the key, which was the biggest mistake.

When it happened, you came to me, embarrassed, but it was too late.

My comfort zone is on the street, lying on a bed of crates.

It didn't have to be this way. I just wanted you to love me.

But every time I start to speak, you say "Wait, I'm too busy."

I don't want to be here on the street; my integrity is gone.

How can I find my way back home?

Can anyone hear me?

My heart is pounding in my chest, don't walk away. Help me!

I want to live and love again!

9

The Abandoned Shack
By The Water Slide

I cannot wait to go down the slide. It excites me more than ever.

The sound of the water trickling down, like rain in bad weather.

The more we visited the site, and happy times grew stronger.

When the park was almost clear, we stayed even longer.

Then I met him, whose eyes were piercing my soul; I could not look away.

My body froze stiff as ice on this beautiful summer day.

He asked me could he hold my hand; I said I was only twelve years old.

Ask my father, I told him, and he said, "He'll say I'm too old."

We met again and again, but no one ever knew.

Then I woke up one day, and my face was black and blue.

I can not come home and live an everyday life again.

I miss the joy and laughter after hanging out with my friends.

Innocence is precious. I am tired of the lies.

Come save me; I'm horrified.

Know one notice the day at the park.

How clever he was that day.

They thought he just a regular guy.

So they all looked away.

How did this happen so quickly?

I became a pregnant child!!!

10

Amber Alert

STOP! Don't do it, do not turn it off.
I want those people to hear it,
Living up there in the loft.
The car pulled out a few minutes ago, speeding down the street,
Headed to the highway while people had a bite to eat.
No one noticed; everything seemed normal to them all.
Little did they know I was in the hands of a criminal.
I heard the alert as my capture sped away.
Not a soul looked up and even stopped to pray.
I trusted you with my life as I daily played in the sand.
But you let me lose my freedom in the arms of a madman.
Here my cry, if I survive, I will never forget your face.
How you ignored the alert, knowing that's the only way I could be traced.
Save me; look for clues.

Don't forget about me.
I deserve to live just like you do.
 I am crying for help in silence!!!

11

I Did Not Want To Do It

I put on my make-up to look good for you,
My red dress with diamonds that match my shoes.
I looked for my purse
And I had this out-burst
Of thoughts going through my head.
The darkness of my thoughts
Wanted me to jump back in bed.
It's ok; you can make it when no one's trying to help.
These thoughts are trying to tell me, "It's ok hurt myself."
I head out the door,
As classy as I can be.
Little do they know, I'm on the edge of sanity.
I entered the party as usual, and everything appeared alright.

11 I DID NOT WANT TO DO IT

Little did they know I would start a vast scene tonight.

Only because I need help, and you all cannot see it or do not care to.
I need COUNSELING!

12

He saw me across the room, finding his new prey,
Setting me up for failure in an unusual way.
You were the only one that mattered in your own mind.
You did not realize what you had, and yes, I was one of a kind.
You took me for granted, and I remained planted in your lies and deceit.
One day I heard a voice that said it was time to be released.
My mind started turning, and I did not know what to do.
But then I began to relax my mind and said this life is not for you.
My future was waiting in the balance; I had to hurry up.
I was not going to wait another minute for God to fill my cup.
I'm free now, I can see now, and just know it's never too late.

Liberate yourself from all that manipulate.

I know you didn't see this coming, and it hurt you to the core.

Don't worry. God saw it all and will give you so much more.

My crushing produced valuable oil that no man could take.

WATCH for the signs. Don't be stupid.

13

In The Gathering

We gather all together, and all hands are lifted high.
One by one, we sang our songs
And then I started to cry.
I got convicted in my heart
And started to walk out the door.
I felt his hands on my shoulder,
Walking me down the corridor.
I screamed with fright and said, "What is this?"
The more I struggled, the more he tightened my wrist.
I looked intently at him and said, "This is a sin."
I noticed his face change and turn as he turned and walked away.
He said, "I can't do this anymore," and changed his life that day.
God stood up in me this day. I do not know why.
But this one got away from the hands of the enemy!

13 IN THE GATHERING

Stop putting these masks on so you can truly see,
The enemy wants to take you from me.
Gathering where they lurk.

14

Set The Record Straight

You don't have a clue what's going on around you.
You are blinded by the smoke; that should have been a clue.
You walk with your nose in the air,
Telling people you don't care
Of what is going on around me.
It is all about me, you see.
I ride in my Tesla,
Refusing to help her.
It is alright with me,
as she sits homeless under that tree.
I don't want to know the outcome of why she lost her home.
You see, it doesn't bother me.

You are stupid; it could be you! SMH fool!

15

Green Lives Matter

Here I am, crying for help.
When all you can see is yourself.
Hidden behind the green
That turned you into a machine.
So focused on the next
Now your mind is perplexed.
Yet craving more
While your child turns into a whore
For years you turned your head
While I slept in many beds.
Who are you to scold me?
When you didn't take the time to hold me
See, it's your fault, and now you want to talk.
The damage has been done; I will come out, but alone!
Thanks, Daddy, your green meant more.

16

Fictitious Harmony

We visited the grocery store.
Coming down the rack,
I pretend to be happy
Because the gun was in my back.
I looked across the store.
I noticed the police in blue.
I couldn't say a thing.
My predator will kill him and me too.
I pray someone will notice
That all this is not real,
And with every step I take,
 he's close on my heels.
Please, God, let someone notice me.
Let them look away from their lives.
For a minute, I am innocent, look
my picture is on the wall.

17

Stop! That's Evidence

What are you doing out there?
Stop sweeping up my hair.
I pulled it from the root,
To give you a closer look.
I even ripped my shirt
And left it near the dirt.
I got some drops of blood.
This was for evidence, you see,
I am doing this to be set free.
Don't mop, sweep, or vacuum
Because that will be my final doom.
Stop and pay attention.
It's 101 comprehensions.
Notice the clues; can you hear us?

18

You Didn't Forget

I see you looking around,
Trying to figure out what happened.
Tears wailing in your eyes
Like drops of rain falling from the sky.
You didn't give up on trying to find me.
You even prayed on that bad knee
For my freedom to come to pass,
Carrying your prayers outside,
Looking for every clue,
Passing the wooded area.
They wanted you to give up and you said never.
You saw the evidence under the broken feather.
The family came together after they got the call
And said we will meet you at city hall.
Thank you for not giving up on me!
You searched and didn't give up.

Praise God! You found me!

,

After reading these poems, I pray we look a little closer at the people and things we tend to overlook or ignore that are clearly seen before us. Just like the man with the infirmity for thirty-eight years: he sat by the water waiting for the angel to come down and stir up the water, and whoever stepped in first would be healed (John 5:1-15). Like us, they saw the evidence, even the signs, but he was overlooked because everyone else was consumed with self. We never know when someone wants to commit suicide or have a mental breakdown. Sometimes it only takes a smile, an open arm, a listening ear, or a dollar bill just to ease the pain of someone. I remember this young lady was acting a little over the top in the doctor's office where I currently work when I wrote this book. I remember talking to her on the phone after her visit to ask a couple of questions; she continued to ask me as well. I answered her questions, but the more I showed compassion, the more open she became. She began to tell me about sequences of things happening in her life, and I began to understand why she acted the way she did; it was a cover-up. Ultimately, I gave an inspiring word of encouragement and prayer because she was under surmountable stress. She just needed someone to listen.

Do not overlook the signs; they are out there. This young woman could have exploded in rage due to circumstances that outweighed her, but the weight was lifted due to a simple compassionate conversation over the phone and a gratitude of thanks.

Can you hear them now?

Take away notes

_____

_____

_____

_____

_____

_____

_____

_____

_____

_____

_____

_____

_____

_____

_____

_____

_____

_____

_____

_____

What would you do now to change your perception of what looks unusual that could turn into tragedy?

_____

_____

_____

_____

_____

_____

_____

_____

_____

_____

_____

_____

_____

_____

_____

_____

_____

_____

_____

For The Road

You watch T.V, change your clothes, and even your identity,
But what will you do if you get a call that it is your family?
Until then, peace!

About The Author

Carol Hurst, the founder of Handsoffire LLC, structures to encourage and use your hands as your voice of healing for the people. She is a certified Life coach, BS in Human Services at Columbia International University, and Author of Loyalty Stained and Poetic Justice Speak. Can they hear us? Carol Hurst is a devoted mother and grandmother. She is a woman that rather be in the background to help shine the light shine on others, but God has other plans. Carol Hurst is a woman that loves God and has compassion for His people. She is dedicated to servanthood and determined to make a change for the greater good.

She prays that this book's purpose will open the eyes of humanity to see the things we miss daily. Let us be a voice to those who have mouths that cannot speak, ears that cannot hear or eyes that cannot see. The evidence is there; stop being consumed with our own thoughts and desires and strategize a plan of action to help those who are crying out to be free. The muted voice screams for help even in the chief concourse. Just look and listen.

Poetic Justice, Speak!